Table of Contents

Tomato Soup 4

Irish Stew in Bread Bowl 6

Chicken and Homemade Noodle Soup 8

Oyster Stew 10

Summer Squash Stew 10

Hot and Sour Soup 12

Catalonian Stew 14

Ground Beef, Spinach and Barley Soup 16

Chicken and Herb Stew 17

French Onion Soup 18

Beef Stew 20

Chunky Chicken Stew 20

Black & White Mexican Bean Soup 22

Hearty Vegetable Stew 24

Italian Mushroom Soup 26

Jamaican Black Bean Stew 28

Cream of Broccoli Soup with Croutons 30

Acknowledgments 30

SOUPS & STEWS

Tomato Soup

  1 tablespoon vegetable oil
  1 cup chopped onion
  2 cloves garlic, coarsely chopped
  ½ cup chopped carrot
  ¼ cup chopped celery
  2 cans (28 ounces each) crushed tomatoes in tomato purée
3½ cups chicken broth
  1 tablespoon Worcestershire sauce
  ½ to 1 teaspoon salt
  ½ teaspoon dried thyme
  ¼ to ½ teaspoon black pepper
  2 to 4 drops hot pepper sauce

1. Heat oil in large saucepan or Dutch oven over medium-high heat. Add onion and garlic; cook and stir 1 to 2 minutes or until onion is tender. Add carrot and celery; cook and stir 7 to 9 minutes or until tender.

2. Stir in tomatoes, broth, Worcestershire sauce, salt, thyme, black pepper and hot pepper sauce. Reduce heat to low. Cover and simmer 20 minutes, stirring frequently.

Makes 6 servings

Note: For smoother soup, remove from heat. Let cool about 10 minutes. Pour soup, in small batches, into food processor or blender; process until smooth. Return soup to saucepan; simmer 3 to 5 minutes or until heated through.

SOUPS & STEWS

Irish Stew in Bread Bowl

- 1½ pounds lean, boned American lamb shoulder, cut into 1-inch cubes
- ¼ cup all-purpose flour
- 2 tablespoons vegetable oil
- 2 cloves garlic, crushed
- 2 cups water
- ¼ cup Burgundy wine
- 5 medium carrots, chopped
- 3 medium potatoes, peeled and sliced
- 2 large onions, peeled and chopped
- 2 ribs celery, sliced
- ¾ teaspoon black pepper
- 1 cube beef bouillon, crushed
- 1 cup frozen peas
- ½ cup sliced fresh mushrooms
- Round bread, unsliced*

*Stew can be served individually in small loaves or in one large loaf. Slice bread crosswise near top to form lid. Hollow larger piece, leaving 1-inch border. Fill "bowl" with hot stew; cover with "lid." Serve immediately.

Coat lamb with flour while heating oil in Dutch oven over low heat. Add lamb and garlic; cook and stir until brown. Add water, wine, carrots, potatoes, onions, celery, pepper and bouillon. Cover; simmer 30 to 35 minutes.

Add peas and mushrooms. Cover; simmer 10 minutes. Bring to a boil; adjust seasonings, if necessary. Serve in bread.

Makes 6 to 8 servings

Favorite recipe from **American Lamb Board**

SOUPS & STEWS

Chicken and Homemade Noodle Soup

¾ cup all-purpose flour
2 teaspoons finely chopped fresh thyme *or* ½ teaspoon dried thyme, divided
¼ teaspoon salt
1 egg yolk, beaten
2 cups plus 3 tablespoons cold water, divided
1 pound boneless skinless chicken thighs, cut into ½- to ¾-inch pieces
5 cups chicken broth
1 onion, chopped
1 carrot, thinly sliced
¾ cup peas
Chopped fresh parsley

1. Stir flour, 1 teaspoon thyme and salt in small bowl. Add egg yolk and 3 tablespoons water; stir until mixed. Shape into small ball. Place dough on lightly floured surface; flatten slightly. Knead 5 minutes or until dough is smooth and elastic, adding more flour to prevent sticking, if necessary. Cover with plastic wrap. Let stand 15 minutes.

2. Roll out dough to ⅛-inch thickness on lightly floured surface. Let dough stand about 30 minutes to dry slightly. Cut into ¼-inch-wide strips. Cut strips 1½ to 2 inches long; set aside.

3. Combine chicken and remaining 2 cups water in medium saucepan. Bring to a boil over high heat. Reduce heat to medium-low; cover and simmer 5 minutes or until chicken is cooked through. Drain chicken.

4. Combine broth, onion, carrot and remaining 1 teaspoon thyme in large saucepan. Bring to a boil over high heat. Add noodles. Reduce heat to medium-low; simmer, uncovered, 8 minutes or until noodles are tender. Stir in chicken and peas; bring to a boil. Sprinkle with parsley. *Makes 4 servings*

Oyster Stew

- 1 quart shucked oysters, with their liquor
- 8 cups milk
- ½ cup (1 stick) margarine, cut into pieces
- 1 teaspoon freshly ground white pepper
- ½ teaspoon salt
- Paprika
- 2 tablespoons finely chopped fresh parsley

Heat oysters in their liquor in medium saucepan over high heat until oyster edges begin to curl, about 2 to 3 minutes. Heat milk and margarine together in large saucepan over medium-high heat just to boiling. Add pepper and salt.

Stir in oysters and their liquor. Do not boil or overcook stew or oysters may get tough. Pour stew into tureen. Dust with paprika; sprinkle with parsley.

Makes 8 servings

Favorite recipe from **National Fisheries Institute**

Summer Squash Stew

- 2 pounds bulk Italian turkey sausage or diced cooked chicken
- 4 cans (about 14 ounces each) diced seasoned tomatoes
- 5 medium yellow squash, thinly sliced
- 5 medium zucchini, thinly sliced
- 1 red onion, finely chopped
- 2 tablespoons Italian seasoning
- 1 tablespoon dried tomato, basil and garlic spice seasoning
- 4 cups (16 ounces) shredded Mexican cheese blend

Slow Cooker Directions

1. Brown sausage in batches 6 to 8 minutes in large nonstick skillet over medium-high heat, stirring to break up meat. Drain fat. Combine sausage, tomatoes, squash, zucchini, onion, Italian seasoning and garlic spice seasoning in 4-quart slow cooker; mix well.

2. Cover; cook on LOW 3 hours. Sprinkle with cheese.

Makes 6 servings

Hot and Sour Soup

1 package (1 ounce) dried shiitake mushrooms
4 ounces firm tofu, drained
4 cups vegetable broth
3 tablespoons white vinegar
2 tablespoons soy sauce
½ to 1 teaspoon hot chili oil
¼ teaspoon white pepper
1 cup shredded cooked pork, chicken or turkey
½ cup drained canned bamboo shoots, cut into thin strips
3 tablespoons water
2 tablespoons cornstarch
1 egg white, lightly beaten
¼ cup thinly sliced green onions or chopped fresh cilantro
1 teaspoon dark sesame oil

1. Place mushrooms in small bowl; cover with warm water. Soak 20 minutes to soften. Drain; squeeze out excess water. Discard stems; slice caps. Press tofu lightly between paper towels; cut into ½-inch squares or triangles.

2. Combine broth, vinegar, soy sauce, chili oil and white pepper in medium saucepan; bring to a boil over high heat. Reduce heat to medium-low; simmer 2 minutes.

3. Stir in mushrooms, tofu, pork and bamboo shoots; cook and stir until heated through.

4. Stir water and cornstarch in small bowl until smooth. Stir into soup until blended. Cook and stir 4 minutes or until soup boils and thickens. Remove from heat.

5. Pour egg white in thin stream into soup, stirring constantly in one direction. Stir in green onions and sesame oil.

Makes 4 servings

SOUPS & STEWS

Catalonian Stew

- 2 boneless skinless chicken breasts, cut into bite-size pieces
- 3 ounces pepperoni, diced
- 1 tablespoon vegetable oil
- 2 cans (15 ounces each) tomato sauce
- 3 cups chicken broth
- 1 cup pimiento-stuffed green olives, halved
- 2 tablespoons sugar
- 8 ounces uncooked rotini or other shaped pasta
- 1/3 cup chopped fresh parsley
- 1/8 teaspoon crushed saffron (optional)
- 1 cup (4 ounces) SARGENTO® Fancy Shredded Mild or Sharp Cheddar Cheese
- 1 cup (4 ounces) SARGENTO® Fancy Shredded Monterey Jack Cheese

In Dutch oven, cook chicken and pepperoni in oil over medium heat until chicken is lightly browned, about 5 minutes; drain. Add tomato sauce, chicken broth, olives and sugar. Bring to a boil; reduce heat and simmer, covered, 15 minutes. Return to a boil. Add rotini, parsley and saffron, if desired; cover and cook an additional 15 minutes or until pasta is tender. Combine Cheddar and Monterey Jack cheeses in small bowl. Spoon stew into 6 individual ovenproof serving bowls; sprinkle evenly with cheese. Bake in preheated 350°F oven about 5 minutes or until cheese is melted.

Makes 6 servings

CATALONIAN STEW

SOUPS & STEWS

Ground Beef, Spinach and Barley Soup

- 12 ounces ground beef
- 4 cups water
- 1 can (about 14 ounces) stewed tomatoes
- 1½ cups thinly sliced carrots
- 1 cup chopped onion
- ½ cup quick-cooking barley
- 1½ teaspoons beef bouillon granules
- 1½ teaspoons dried thyme
- 1 teaspoon dried oregano
- ½ teaspoon garlic powder
- ¼ teaspoon black pepper
- ⅛ teaspoon salt
- 3 cups torn stemmed spinach

1. Brown beef 6 to 8 minutes in large saucepan over medium-high heat, stirring to break up meat. Rinse beef under warm water; drain.

2. Return beef to saucepan. Stir in water, tomatoes, carrots, onion, barley, bouillon, thyme, oregano, garlic powder, pepper and salt; bring to a boil over high heat.

3. Reduce heat to medium-low. Cover; simmer 12 to 15 minutes or until barley and vegetables are tender, stirring occasionally. Stir in spinach; cook until spinach starts to wilt.

Makes 4 servings

SOUPS & STEWS

Chicken and Herb Stew

½ cup all-purpose flour
½ teaspoon salt
¼ teaspoon paprika
¼ teaspoon black pepper
4 chicken drumsticks
4 chicken thighs
2 tablespoons olive oil
12 ounces new potatoes, quartered
2 carrots, quartered lengthwise and cut into 3-inch pieces
1 green bell pepper, cut into thin strips
¾ cup chopped onion
2 cloves garlic, minced
1¾ cups water
¼ cup dry white wine
2 cubes chicken bouillon
1 tablespoon chopped fresh oregano
1 teaspoon chopped fresh rosemary
2 tablespoons chopped fresh Italian parsley (optional)

1. Combine flour, salt, paprika and black pepper in shallow dish; stir until well blended. Coat chicken with flour mixture; shake off excess.

2. Heat oil in large skillet over medium-high heat. Add chicken; cook 8 minutes or until brown on both sides, turning once. Transfer to plate.

3. Add potatoes, carrots, bell pepper, onion and garlic to skillet; cook and stir 5 minutes or until lightly browned. Add water, wine and bouillon; cook 1 minute, stirring to scrape up browned bits. Stir in oregano and rosemary.

4. Place chicken on top of vegetable mixture, turning several times to coat. Cover; simmer 45 to 50 minutes or until chicken is cooked through (165°F), turning occasionally. Garnish with parsley.

Makes 4 servings

SOUPS & STEWS

French Onion Soup

   1 tablespoon vegetable oil
2½ large onions, halved and thinly sliced (about 2½ cups)*
  ¼ teaspoon sugar
   2 tablespoons all-purpose flour
3½ cups SWANSON® Beef Broth (Regular, Lower Sodium or Certified Organic)
  ¼ cup dry white wine or vermouth
   4 slices French bread, toasted**
  ½ cup shredded Swiss cheese

*Use a food processor with slicing attachment for ease in preparation.
**For even more flavor, try rubbing the bread with a garlic clove and topping it with the cheese before toasting.

1. Heat the oil in a 4-quart saucepot over medium heat. Add the onions. Reduce the heat to low. Cover and cook for 15 minutes. Uncover the saucepot.

2. Increase the heat to medium. Add the sugar and cook for 15 minutes or until the onions are golden.

3. Stir the flour in the saucepot and cook and stir for 1 minute. Stir in the broth and wine. Heat to a boil. Reduce the heat to low. Cook for 10 minutes.

4. Divide the soup among **4** bowls. Top **each** with a bread slice and cheese. *Makes 4 servings*

Prep Time: 10 minutes
Cook Time: 45 minutes
Total Time: 55 minutes

FRENCH ONION SOUP

SOUPS & STEWS

Beef Stew

> 5 potatoes, diced
> 5 carrots, cut into bite-size pieces
> 3 pounds beef stew meat
> 4 onions, quartered
> 2 stalks celery, chopped
> 1 can (about 28 ounces) diced tomatoes
> 1½ cups water
> 1 tablespoon plus 1½ teaspoons salt
> 1½ teaspoons *each* paprika and Worcestershire sauce
> ¾ teaspoon black pepper
> 1 clove garlic, minced
> 1 bay leaf

Slow Cooker Directions

1. Layer potatoes, carrots, beef, onions, celery and tomatoes in 5-quart slow cooker. Stir water, salt, paprika, Worcestershire sauce, pepper, garlic and bay leaf in medium bowl until well blended. Add to slow cooker.

2. Cover; cook on LOW 10 to 12 hours. *Makes 8 servings*

Chunky Chicken Stew

> 1 teaspoon olive oil
> 1 small onion, chopped
> 1 cup *each* thinly sliced carrots and chicken broth
> 1 can (about 14 ounces) diced tomatoes
> 1 cup diced cooked chicken breast
> 3 cups sliced kale or baby spinach

1. Heat oil in large saucepan over medium-high heat. Add onion; cook and stir about 5 minutes or until golden brown. Stir in carrots and broth; bring to a boil. Reduce heat; simmer, uncovered, 5 minutes.

2. Stir in tomatoes; simmer 5 minutes or until carrots are tender. Add chicken; cook and stir until heated through. Add kale; stir until wilted. *Makes 2 servings*

BEEF STEW

Black & White Mexican Bean Soup

- 1 tablespoon vegetable oil
- 1 cup chopped onion
- ½ teaspoon POLANER® Minced Garlic
- ¼ cup all-purpose flour
- 1 packet (1.25 ounces) ORTEGA® Taco Seasoning Mix
- 2 cups milk
- 1 can (about 14 ounces) chicken broth
- 1 package (16 ounces) frozen corn
- 1 can (15 ounces) JOAN OF ARC® Great Northern Beans, rinsed, drained
- 1 can (15 ounces) ORTEGA® Black Beans, rinsed, drained
- 1 can (4 ounces) ORTEGA® Fire-Roasted Diced Green Chiles
- 2 tablespoons chopped cilantro

HEAT oil in large pan or Dutch oven over medium-high heat. Add onion and garlic; cook until onion is tender.

STIR in flour and taco seasoning mix; gradually stir in milk until blended. Add chicken broth, corn, beans and chiles.

BRING to a boil, stirring constantly. Reduce heat to low; simmer 15 minutes or until thickened, stirring occasionally.

STIR in cilantro.

Makes 6 servings

Hearty Vegetable Stew

- 1 tablespoon olive oil
- 1 cup chopped onion
- ¾ cup chopped carrots
- 3 cloves garlic, minced
- 4 cups coarsely chopped green cabbage
- 3½ cups coarsely chopped unpeeled new red potatoes
- 1 teaspoon salt
- 1 teaspoon dried rosemary
- ½ teaspoon black pepper
- 4 cups vegetable broth
- 1 can (about 15 ounces) Great Northern beans, rinsed and drained
- 1 can (about 14 ounces) diced tomatoes
- Grated Parmesan cheese (optional)

1. Heat oil in large saucepan over medium-high heat. Add onion and carrots; cook and stir 3 minutes. Add garlic; cook and stir 1 minute.

2. Add cabbage, potatoes, salt, rosemary and pepper; cook 1 minute. Stir in broth, beans and tomatoes; bring to a boil. Reduce heat to medium-low; simmer 15 minutes or until potatoes are tender. Sprinkle with cheese, if desired.

Makes about 7 servings

Italian Mushroom Soup

½ cup dried porcini mushrooms (about ½ ounce)
1 tablespoon olive oil
2 cups chopped onions
8 ounces sliced cremini or button mushrooms
2 cloves garlic, minced
¼ teaspoon dried thyme
¼ cup all-purpose flour
4 cups vegetable broth
½ cup whipping cream
⅓ cup Marsala wine (optional)
Salt and black pepper

1. Place dried mushrooms in small bowl; cover with boiling water. Let stand 15 minutes or until tender.

2. Meanwhile, heat oil in large saucepan over medium heat. Add onions; cook 5 minutes or until translucent, stirring occasionally. Add cremini mushrooms, garlic and thyme; cook 8 minutes, stirring occasionally. Add flour; cook and stir 1 minute. Stir in broth.

3. Drain mushrooms, reserving liquid. Chop mushrooms; add to saucepan with reserved liquid. Bring to a boil. Reduce heat to medium-low; simmer 10 minutes.

4. Stir in cream and wine. Season with salt and pepper. Simmer 5 minutes or until heated through. *Makes 6 to 8 servings*

Jamaican Black Bean Stew

  2 cups uncooked brown rice
  2 pounds sweet potatoes
  3 pounds butternut squash
  1 can (about 14 ounces) vegetable broth
  1 large onion, coarsely chopped
  3 cloves garlic, minced
  1 tablespoon curry powder
1½ teaspoons ground allspice
  ½ teaspoon ground red pepper
  ¼ teaspoon salt
  2 cans (about 15 ounces each) black beans, rinsed and drained
  ½ cup raisins
  3 tablespoons fresh lime juice
  1 cup diced tomato
  1 cup diced peeled cucumber

1. Prepare rice according to package directions.

2. Meanwhile, peel sweet potatoes; cut into ¾-inch chunks to measure 4 cups. Peel squash; remove seeds. Cut into ¾-inch cubes to measure 5 cups.

3. Combine sweet potatoes, squash, broth, onion, garlic, curry powder, allspice, red pepper and salt in Dutch oven. Bring to a boil; reduce heat to low. Cover and simmer 15 minutes or until sweet potatoes and squash are tender.

4. Add beans and raisins; simmer 5 minutes or until heated through. Stir in lime juice. Serve stew over brown rice; top with tomato and cucumber. *Makes 8 servings*

SOUPS & STEWS

Cream of Broccoli Soup with Croutons

   3 tablespoons butter, divided
   3 cups French or rustic bread, cut into ½-inch cubes
   ¼ cup grated Parmesan cheese
   1 tablespoon olive oil
   1 large onion, chopped
   8 cups (about 1½ pounds) chopped broccoli
   3 cups chicken broth
   1 cup whipping cream or half-and-half
      Salt and black pepper

1. Preheat oven to 350°F.

2. Melt 1 tablespoon butter in small microwavable bowl. Add bread cubes, cheese and oil; toss to combine. Transfer to 15×10-inch jelly-roll pan. Bake 12 to 14 minutes or until golden brown, stirring once. Cool completely.

3. Melt remaining 2 tablespoons butter in large saucepan over medium heat. Add onion; cook and stir 5 minutes. Add broccoli and broth; cover and bring to a boil over high heat. Reduce heat; simmer 25 minutes or until broccoli is tender. Cool 10 minutes.

4. Transfer soup in batches to blender; blend until smooth. Return to saucepan. Stir in cream, salt and pepper; cook until heated through. *Do not boil.* Top with croutons.   *Makes 8 servings*

ACKNOWLEDGMENTS

The publisher would like to thank the companies and organizations listed below for the use of their recipes and photographs in this publication.

American Lamb Board

Campbell Soup Company

National Fisheries Institute

Ortega®, A Division of B&G Foods, Inc.

Sargento® Foods Inc.